SHOULD A
CHRISTIAN
BE A MASON?

PASTOR KEVIN
(509) 697-7833

DAVID W. DANIELS
ILLUSTRATED BY DEBORAH DANIELS

CHICK
PUBLICATIONS

For a complete list of distributors near you,
call (909) 987-0771, or visit www.chick.com

Published by:

CHICK PUBLICATIONS
PO Box 3500, Ontario, Calif. 91761-1019 USA
Tel: (909) 987-0771
Fax: (909) 941-8128
Web: www.chick.com
Email: postmaster@chick.com

Printed in the United States of America

Fourth Printing

ISBN: 978-07589-0781-3

If you are a Mason,
or are thinking of becoming one…

If you are not a Mason,
but want to understand Masonry
in the light of Christianity
and the Bible…

If you are a Christian,
and you think Masonry is
completely compatible with
Bible-believing Christianity…

This book is for you.

This book has a very specific purpose: It will help you to find out what Masonry believes, compared to what the Bible says.

For Christians, the Bible is our only reliable source to learn who God is, and what He wants for us, including how to get our sins forgiven and have eternal life in heaven with Him.

I want you, my brother or sister in Christ, whether a Mason or not, to be able to answer this question with confidence and understanding:

"Should a Christian be a Mason?"

To do that, we need to find out these things:

• Where did Masonry come from?
• What do Masons believe?
• Who can we trust for our information?
• Who is God, according to these trusted authorities?
• Is the God of the Bible the same as the god of Masonry?

By the end of this book you will be able to answer these questions for yourself.

God bless you as you read.

CONTENTS

CHAPTER 1

◆

MASONRY'S SECRET ORIGIN

With so many books available on Masonry, [1] you would think it would be a simple thing to discover where Masonic groups came from and what they believe. But that couldn't be further from the truth.

First of all, non-stone-working Masonry by its own admission is "a society of secrets" [2] that has existed in some form at least since the late 1600s. But I've been amazed at how little Masons seem to know about the origin or authoritative beliefs of their own society.

Let's start with where Masonry came from. There are many different opinions. Albert Pike, 33° (33rd degree) Sovereign Grand Commander of the Scottish Rite's Southern Jurisdiction [3] from 1859-1891, seemed to imply that a religious form of Masonry went all the way back to Gautama Buddha (6th-5th centuries BC):

---

1) The terms "Masonry" and "Freemasonry" are treated in this book as having the same meaning.
2) L.C. Helms, *A Modern Mason Examines His Craft: Fact vs. Fiction (Richmond, VA: Macoy Publishing & Masonic Supply Company, Inc., 1981), p. 1.*
3) Presently, the Southern Jurisdiction of the Scottish Rite covers 35 U.S. states, all but 15 in the northeast. The rest are known as the Northern Jurisdiction.

The first Masonic Legislator whose memory is preserved to us by history, was Buddha, who, about a thousand years before the Christian era, reformed the religion of Manous. [4]

That would be extremely helpful for finding the origin of Masonry, if it were proved true. But in reality Pike gives absolutely no documentation at all for this claim—and there is a lot of disagreement about how Masonry formed.

Various Masons have taught that "the Craft"[5] in its modern "speculative" form—something other than "operative Masons," a society of stonemasons—goes back to Rosslyn Chapel,[6] the Druids, the apostle John, John the Baptist, King Solomon, Noah or even Adam.[7] Everyone seems to have a different opinion.

One intriguing theory suggests that the Masons came from Ionian architects, ancient Greek architects who had their own secret society. R. Swineburne Clymer reasoned in his book *Ancient Mystic Oriental Masonry*:

If it be possible to prove the identity of any two societies, from the coincidence of their external forms, we are authorized to conclude that the Fraternity of Ionian architects and

---

4) Albert Pike, *Morals and Dogma of the Ancient and Accepted Scottish Rite of Freemasonry* (Charleston, NC: 1871, 1906. 1949 reprint), p. 277.
5) "The Craft" is another name for Masonry.
6) People like Dr. Robert Lomas hold this theory. See www.robertlomas.com
7) See www.masonicworld.com/education under "About Freemasonry."

the Fraternity of Freemasons are exactly the same... [8]

But which theory is correct? John Hamill, Librarian of the United Grand Lodge of England and author of many Masonic history books, confessed:

When, why and where did Freemasonry originate? There is one answer to these questions: We do not know, despite all the paper and ink that has been expended in examining them...

...Whether we shall ever discover the true origins of Freemasonry is open to question. [9]

Even prominent Satanist, occultist, —and Mason— Aleister Crowley (1875-1947), tried to figure it out. He revealed what he had learned in his autobiography:

We are brought at last face to face with the fundamental problem of the masonic[10] historian —the origin of the whole business. Without any hesitation at all, one may confess that on this critical question nothing is certainly known. [11]

---

8) R. Swineburne Clymer, *Ancient Mystic Oriental Masonry* (1907), p. 77. See also Hyppolyto Joseph da Costa, *The Dionysian Artificers* (1820).

9) John Hamill, *The Craft, a History of English Freemasonry* (Bedfordshire, England: Crucible Books, 1986), pp. 15, 29.

10) In quotes, terms for Masonry are frequently not capitalized. I kept the quotations as the authors originally wrote them. Otherwise I capitalize terms the way Masons generally do.

11) *The Confessions of Aleister Crowley*, (1929, 1969) Part 5, Chapter 72, p. 697. Available online at: www.hermetic.com/crowley/confessions/index.html

So what do we know about Masonic origins? Masons were originally qualified, active stone-workers from guilds in England and Scotland. They crafted beautiful buildings for centuries, up until the late 1500s. It was painstaking work. A mistake in design, measurement or building could cost lives. So they had secret signs only taught to people who had reached that level of expertise. That way a contractor would know he had knowledgeable craftsmen working on the building, even if they had never met before. Or he would know that an apprentice had gained further mastery since the last time they worked together.

But this society of craftsmen changed after the last of the stone cathedrals was built. There was no more work, and so no reason to pass down the knowledge and skills of their craft.

That was pretty much the end of stone-working masons and their guilds. It is said that about that time, rich upper-class males, who liked the idea of a secret society, started joining these remaining "Operative Masons." They were received as "Accepted Masons," and soon they changed the group into what many say was something of a gentlemen's club.

But what about the modern, "Speculative Masonry" that we see in Masonic Halls [12] all over the globe? Most agree it started formally in the Grand Lodge of England

12) Masonic Halls are also called Lodges or Temples. But a Lodge is properly a meeting of Masons, not the building itself.

in 1717. Then the members, primarily "Accepted" Masons, were now philosophers in a fraternity, not actual stonemasons in a guild.

Beyond those accepted facts, the origins of Masonry are shrouded in secrecy.

So where did Masonry come from? After reading seemingly endless Masonic documents and books honestly and faithfully, the best answer I can give you is this:

"Either nobody knows, or nobody is telling."

Doesn't that make you wonder what's going on? Somebody *must know, right?* If so, why hide where Masonry came from? And why would a Christian want be a part of this secretive group? Are there some beliefs in Masonry that attract Christians?

◆

CHAPTER 2

MASONIC BELIEFS EXPOSED

There are books on Masonry in almost every language, both official and unofficial.

- Do they have an agreed-upon set of beliefs?
- Is there an agreed-upon meaning of Masonic symbols, which abound in every Masonic setting?
- What about the meaning of Masonry itself? Can we settle upon one definition and say, "This is Masonry?"

Non-Masonic author Steven Knight was quoted approvingly by Masons when he stated:

> There is therefore *no authoritative state-ment* of what Masons believe or what the Brotherhood stands for in the first, second and third degrees, to which the vast majority of members restrict themselves. Even a 33° Mason who has persevered to attain all the enlightenment that Freemasonry claims to offer could not —even if he were freed from his oath of secrecy— provide more than a purely personal view of the masonic message and the meaning to be attached to masonic

symbolism, since this remains essentially subjective. [13]

If Masonic symbolism is "essentially subjective," then
it is up to the Mason to decide what each symbol means.
This is consistent with what Masonic books say. But is
there at least one correct or "deeper" meaning to these
symbols? That's what this book was written to find out.

The "Blue Degrees"

Masons of all kinds do have certain things in common. Every accepted Candidate starts out as a "Craft,"
"Blue Lodge" or "Ancient Craft" Mason. [14] There are only
three stages or degrees in regular Masonry: he is "initiated" as an Entered Apprentice, "passed" to the Fellowcraft
(2nd) degree and "raised to the sublime (3rd) degree" of
Master Mason.

This whole process of memorizing ritual words and
body movements, as well as other duties, usually takes a
few months. The vast majority don't go any further than
these three Blue Degrees of the Masonic Lodge. As the
unified Grand Lodge of London stated:

> By the solemn Act of Union between the two
> Grand Lodges of Free-masons of England
> in December, 1813, it was "declared and

---

13) Stephen Knight, *The Brotherhood: The Secret World of the Freemasons*
(New York: Dorset Press, 1984), p. 16. (Emphasis mine.)
14) These three Lodges, the Craft Lodge, Blue Lodge and Ancient Craft
Lodge are groups only concerned with the first three degrees of Masonry.

pronounced that pure Antient [sic] Masonry consists of three degrees and no more, viz., those of the Entered Apprentice, the Fellow Craft, and the Master Mason…"[15]

Appendant Bodies

That is true. But beyond that are groups called "appendant bodies," that introduce 3rd degree (3°) Masons to "greater mysteries" and higher degrees. Two of the most well-known, if not the largest, are the Scottish Rite and the York Rite. The York Rite has an additional seven degrees and three "orders," for a total of 13 levels, [16] and the Scottish Rite offers 30 more advanced degrees, including an honorary degree, for a total of 33.

So while there are only three "blue degrees" of the Masonic Lodge, there are a great many more steps for the Mason who wants to "learn about his craft."

In the past, moving up the degrees took years, with much study and memorization involved. But in recent decades, present and former Masons have stated openly that the York Rite degrees can be conferred in many places in a few months; and some degrees, of either York or Scottish Rites, can be received in only a few weeks.

15) John Hervey, Grand Secretary, *Constitutions of the Antient [sic] Fraternity of Free and Accepted Masons, Containing the Charges, Regulations, etc., etc.,* (London: Harrison & Sons, 1873), p. 16.
16) With two exceptions: some councils add the Most Excellent Master degree to Cryptic Masonry, and there is The Passing Order of St. Paul in the Order of Knights Templar.

The "Landmarks" of Masonry

All Masons have a few other things in common. They call these the "Landmarks" of Masonry. We have already mentioned the three degrees in every single Masonic order: *Entered Apprentice, Fellow Craft* and *Master Mason*. The following are also essential to Masonry:

• **The Legend of Hiram Abiff:** This is the non-biblical teaching that Solomon had a special Grand Master builder for the temple in Jerusalem. According to the legend (adapted from many ancient myths) he was killed by three men, buried west of Jerusalem, then raised from the dead (or disinterred [17] and transplanted – interpretations vary). This made-up modern myth is regularly repeated as the central ceremony for receiving the 3rd degree (3°).

• **The "Three Great Lights:"** These must be present in any Masonic meeting. They are:

1) **The Volume of Sacred Law (VSL):** This is any sacred writing of a religion that has at least one god and contains some sort of morality.

2) **The Compasses:** The upside-down "V"-shaped device that draws circles.

3) **The Square:** The "L"-shaped instrument used to measure or draw right angles.

One Masonic writer describes their use this way:

---

17) This means they dug up the body and removed it from the grave.

> As the VSL is not read in our Lodges, its teachings per se are of no consequence. It is a symbol and a symbol only, and it is shown as supporting the other two symbols, the Square and Compasses. [18]

So what's the point of having the Bible (or other VSL) there in the first place? Maybe the Bible is there to make Christians think that Masonry is compatible with Christianity. After all, they freely give a Masonic Bible to professing Christians who ask for them.

So let's use that Masonic Bible to find out who Masons trust for information about Masonry.

---

18) From the article "The Volume of Sacred Law," in The Masonic Trowel, at www.the masonictrowel.com.

CHAPTER 3

———— ◆ ————

WHO WILL YOU TRUST?

As you have seen, one of the three "Great Lights" of Masonry is often said to be the Bible. When a friend of mine became a Christian and left both Islam and Masonry, he lent me his Masonic Bible to investigate. (It's entitled, "The Holy Bible: The Great Light in Masonry.")

Later I acquired two other Masonic Bibles for comparison. One turned out to be identical to my friend's; the other had a number of differences. They are both King James Bibles, but they have variations in the additional material bound together with the scriptures. And all of that material is important.

If you are going to publish a Bible, you know it is considered the words of God, so anything you add to that book must be the most important, widely-accepted information you can think of. You will only put in items that are supposed to have great significance to those who will own it. So you must think a lot about which authors to use, before you add their writings to the pages of the Holy

19

Bible. Here's a glance at what these publishers[19] thought was important enough to be included.

In one Masonic Bible I found:

- John Wesley Kelchner's "The Bible and King Solomon's Temple in Masonry."

- CE Patterson's compilation of 160 Masonic Questions and Answers from the writings of Albert G. Mackey.

- Joseph Fort Newton's "The Words of a Great Masonic Divine"

In the other Masonic Bible I discovered:

- Record pages for both Scottish Rite and York Rite.

- S.J. Pridgen's compilation of 215 Symbolic Masonry Questions and Answers from the writings of Charles H. Merz.

- C.H. Stauffacher and Charles P. Roney's Biblical Index to Freemasonry.

- Plus sections on:
  - The three Blue Lodge degrees.
  - The 7 main degrees and 3 orders in the York Rite.
  - The 30 degrees of the Scottish Rite.

Every word on the three main degrees, as well

---

19) The publishers were the AJ Holman Company for my friend's Bible, and both the John A. Hertel Co. and DeVore & Sons, Inc. for the other (this edition was published by Heirloom Bible Publishers, www.masonicbibles.com).

as those of the York and Scottish Rites, was a direct quote out of Albert Pike's 1871 book, *Morals and Dogma of the Ancient and Accepted Scottish Rite of Freemasonry* (usually abbreviated *Morals and Dogma*). [20]

These people, whose writings are in Masonic Bibles (Joseph Fort Newton, Kelchner, Merz, Patterson, Pridgen, Roney, Stauffacher, Albert G. Mackey and Albert Pike) are held in very high esteem by the Masonic community in general. Don't let anybody fool you.

So what can we learn of Masonry from these men? Let's pick a couple, starting with Joseph Fort Newton.

Joseph Fort Newton

20) I have scanned copies of the 1874, 1906 and 1949 printings and have not discerned any differences between them.

Here is some of what Newton wrote, found in my friend's Masonic Bible.

> Thus, by the very honor which Masonry pays to the Bible, it teaches us to *revere every book of faith* in which men find help for today and hope for the morrow, joining hands with the man of Islam as he takes oath on *the Koran,* [21] and with the *Hindu* as he makes covenant with God upon the book that he loves best.

> For Masonry knows, what so many forget, that *religions are many, but Religion is one...* Therefore, it invites to its altar men of all faiths, knowing that, if they use different names for "the Nameless One of a hundred names," they are yet praying to the one God and Father of all; knowing, also, that while they read different volumes, they are in fact reading *the same vast Book of the Faith of Man* as revealed in the struggle and sorrow of the race in its quest of God. So that, great and noble as the Bible is, Masonry sees it as a symbol of that eternal Book of the Will of God... [22]

Look carefully. Newton didn't speak for just the "Blue Lodge," or the Scottish or York Rite. He said here

---

21) The Koran is the same holy book of Islam that is now spelled Qur'an.
22) "The Words of a Great Masonic Divine: The Bible in Masonry" in *The Holy Bible: the Great Light in Masonry*, Masonic edition, Temple-Illustrated (Philadelphia, PA: AJ Holman Co., 1924-1957), pp. 3-4. (Emphasis mine.)

that Masonry teaches Masons to revere the Qur'an, a book which commands the death, dismemberment or other violent actions toward those who reject the message of Islamic invaders. [23]

He said it teaches Masons to revere the Hindu book (most often meaning the Bhagavad Gita), which claims to be a conversation between the pagan god Krishna and Arjuna, a warrior, about the duties of war and the philosophies of Yoga and Vedanta. [24]

Is Newton saying that all these gods are the same? And that these books are equal to the Bible? And that therefore all theistic[25] religions are equal? And that all Masons are supposed to believe this? Yes! In fact, according to Roy L. Demming, S.W., of the Utah Research Lodge:

> If the Old and New Testaments of the Holy Bible are to be taken as separate Volumes, there are no fewer than *seven sets of Holy Writings* in use in the Lodges of the East, in the band of countries stretching from Israel to New Zealand. These are:

23) See Mohammad Al Ghazoli, *Christ, Muhammad and I*. Available from Chick Publications.
24) Vedanta teaches the lie that human nature is actually divine and one's aim in life is to realize this. Then one may attain "cosmic consciousness," or "self-realization." But the Bible says our heart is wicked (Jeremiah 17:9) and self-realization is foolishness (Proverbs 18:2 – the KJV is especially clear).
25) Theistic means believing in at least one god, one of which is usually supreme.

1. The Bible (Old Testament) for Hebrews.
2. The Bible (Old and New Testaments) for Christians.
3. The Dhammapadra for the Mahayana Sect of Buddhists.
4. The [Bhagavad] Gita for Hindus.
5. The Granth Sahib for Sikhs.
6. The Koran for Muslims.
7. The Zend Avesta for Parsees and Zoroastrians.

All of these Sacred Books Allude to a Supreme Deity. [26]

That is about all they have in common: they "allude to a supreme deity." All those books (other than the Bible) may talk about a supreme god of some sort (which includes people who believe that humanity is divine), but their god is *not* the God of the Bible. They are *not* equal.

Look at what God says in His word, the Holy Bible:

To whom then will ye liken me, or shall I be equal? saith the Holy One. [27]

To whom will ye liken me, and make me equal, and compare me, that we may be like? [28]

The answer to both is, "*no one*." God declares in the

---

26) Roy L. Demming, "The Great Lights in the East," SW, Utah Research Lodge (Utah: The Beehive State Trestleboard, Feb. 1996), found at www.themasonictrowel.com. (Emphasis and clarification mine.)
27) Isaiah 40:25.
28) Isaiah 46:5.

Bible that He cannot be likened to, or compared to, anyone, god or man.

You are welcome to look up all the Bible verses I present in this book. I did, in a KJV Masonic Bible. They're right there in plain sight for any Mason who has the courage to look them up.

Now let's turn over to Isaiah 48:11-12:

> ...I will not give my glory unto another... I
> am he; I am the first, I also am the last. [29]

The Lord God will not share His glory with anyone. The Lord is not like any man-made god or idol or spirit. He is the eternal God, the One and Only God of the universe.

God's own words in the Bible totally contradict these Masonic additions to the Bible. Maybe that's the real reason why the Bible is covered by the compasses and square during their Lodge meetings. Maybe it symbolizes that they should not read the Bible, unless it is through the lenses of Masonry.

Albert Pike

Now let's turn to the mastermind whose description of the degrees and orders of Masonry, including both York and Scottish Rites, was seen as so important that *24 pages* in a Masonic Bible were *direct quotes* of Pike.

---

29) Isaiah 48:11-12.

Albert Pike

Amazingly, though this Masonic Bible quoted his exact words, and it has been approved for and used by both the Scottish and York Rites, Masonic leadership has continually disclaimed Albert Pike's writings since the 1870s. They say it's because neither Pike nor anyone else can "speak for Masonry:"

> Within our Fraternity no one person can speak for Masonry. A Grand Master can speak on organizational matters within his Jurisdiction, just as the Grand Commander can speak on organizational matters within the Southern Jurisdiction of the Scottish Rite. But no one —not a Grand Master, not a Grand Commander, not Albert Pike

himself— can speak for Masonry when it comes to the meanings of its teachings. That is something each Mason must seek and find for himself. No one can speak for Freemasonry. [30]

However, the authors did make an exception:

Unless formally endorsed by action of a grand lodge, no writer can speak for Masonry, only for himself. [31]

What do these statements mean? For starters, let's look at the disclaimer in the middle of the Preface to his 1871 book, *Morals and Dogma*, from my 1874 edition (and every edition after it):

Every one [sic] is entirely free to reject and dissent from whatsoever herein may seem to him to be untrue or unsound. It is only required of him that he shall weigh what is taught, and give it fair hearing and unprejudiced judgment. [32]

This disclaimer is repeated exactly in the analysis and summary of Pike's system of Masonic degrees called *A Bridge to Light*. [33] But that's not all.

---

30) Arturo de Hoyos and S. Brent Morris, *Is It True What They Say About Freemasonry? The Methods of Anti-Masons*, 2nd edition, revised, (Silver Spring, MD: Masonic Information Center, 1993, 1997), Addendum.
31) de Hoyos and Morris, *Is It True What They Say About Freemasonry?* Chapter 1. (Emphasis mine.)
32) *Morals and Dogma* (1874), Preface, p. iv.
33) *A Bridge to Light*, 2nd edition (1995), p. iii; 3rd edition (2006), p. iii.

In the age of the Internet, modern Masonic web pages spend a good deal of time distancing themselves from Pike and his writings. For instance, one web page[34] distances all Masonry from Pike with words like these:

> ...It [Pike's book, *Morals and Dogma*] was NOT important because it was a 'guide' or 'rulebook' of any kind in Freemasonry. It was, simply, the sometimes jumbled thoughts of one man.

The Morals and Dogma of Freemasonry? NO!

> ...For about 60 years *Morals and Dogma* was given as a gift to all who joined the Southern United States jurisdiction of the Scottish Rite. The Scottish Rite is an appendant body of Freemasonry. It is NOT Freemasonry itself! While all Scottish Rite members are Masons less than 25% of Masons have ever been Scottish Rite members.

But wait. Whether someone has attained the degrees in the Scottish Rite is not the issue here. What we want are answers to our basic questions regarding the meaning and beliefs of Masonry.

If a book is accurate, it doesn't matter how many people read it. It is still accurate. So it doesn't matter if only a small percentage of Masons actually reads or understands

---

34) www.masonicinfo.com, which seems to be maintained by Edward L. King.

Pike's huge *Morals and Dogma* or the deeper meaning to the Pike Masonic Ritual. It only matters whether his interpretation truly reveals the meanings of the symbols and elements of Masonry in a way that other Masons generally accept.

If Pike's writings accurately describe Masonic symbols and basic beliefs, then we will be able to better answer the question, should a Christian be a Mason, by examining both Pike's writings and the people who have authoritatively utilized them. The more that influential Masons lift up Pike's writing, the more we can trust that Pike's words (as modified in the newest publications by modern leaders) represent Masonry as understood by its leadership.

If I want to understand Mormonism, I cannot simply talk to a bunch of Mormons down the street. Who knows whether what they believe is official Mormon doctrine?

What I must do instead is read the writings and approved teachings of the Mormon leadership, the "General Authorities," as they're called. What do they teach their own leaders? That helps define Mormon belief more correctly.

In the same way, we need to see how Masonic leadership has used, modified or passed on Pike's teachings. That will show us what Masonic leaders have thought about Albert Pike, *Morals and Dogma*, *A Bridge to Light*, or any book Pike originally wrote.

Then we can see how influential Albert Pike's teachings truly are among Masons. That will also tell us what a Christian will be taught if he enters a Lodge and moves up the degrees of Masonry.

So let's take a look at a few examples of how Pike's teachings are treated by Masonic leadership. As we have already noted, the Heirloom Bible Publishers' Masonic Bible directly quotes from Pike's *Morals and Dogma* for 24 pages to describe the Blue Degrees (the 3 degrees of all Masonic Lodges), as well as those advanced degrees of the York and Scottish Rites.

Arturo de Hoyos

Masonic Grand Archivist and Grand Historian Arturo de Hoyos 33°, the newest editor to *A Bridge to Light* and co-author of *Is It True What They Say About Freemasonry?*[35] was asked: "If you had to pick, what's the one book *every* Mason should read?" De Hoyos responded:

> Jason, I'm a bibliophile, so that's an unfair question. Let me offer three: Bernard E. Jones, *Freemasons' Guide and Compendium*; Albert Pike, *Esoterika;* Henry Coil, *Masonic Encyclopedia*. Read them until you have them *memorized*. Then ask me again, I'll offer you 50 more books.[36]

It sounds like Jones, Pike and Coil come highly recommended. The book by Pike that de Hoyos mentioned is a long-unpublished book that he edited, called *Esoterika: the Symbolism of the Blue Degrees of Freemasonry.*[37] Remember that the "Blue Degrees" are taken by every Mason in the world. Arturo de Hoyos says "every Mason should read" it… "until you have [it] memorized."

Don't let anyone fool you into thinking that Pike wasn't trying to speak for all Masonry. But this shows it's not only Pike. Arturo de Hoyos himself recommends Pike to "every Mason." There's no getting around that fact.

35) Arturo de Hoyos and S Brent Morris, *Is It True What They Say About Freemasonry? The Methods of Anti-Masons* (2nd edition, Revised), (Silver Spring, MD: Masonic Information Center, 1993, 1997).

36) "From the Drafting Table: An Interview with Arturo de Hoyos," Blueprints of the Master Craftsman, Vol. 1, No. 2 (The Supreme Council, 33°, A[ncient] & A[ccepted] S[cottish] R[ite] of Freemasonry, S[outhern] J[urisdiction], USA), p. 2. (Emphasis mine.)

37) Albert Pike, edited by Arturo de Hoyos, *Esoterika: the Symbolism of the Blue Degrees of Freemasonry,* (Scottish Rite Research Society, 2nd edition, 2008).

Anyone who has taken those first three "Blue Degrees" is invited to learn about the Scottish Rite's additional 30 degrees through the "Scottish Rite Master Craftsman Program." It's a course where you can learn at your own pace, reading two specific books and taking a number of open-book tests. Can you guess who wrote the initial forms of *both* required books? That's right: Albert Pike. Here it is from their own website:

> The Scottish Rite Master Craftsman (SRMC) program is an exciting by-mail correspondence course designed and administered by staff at the House of the Temple in Washington, D.C., under the guidance and leadership of the Supreme Council, 33°, of the A. & A. Scottish Rite, Southern Jurisdiction, U.S.A. Consisting of six lessons, it utilizes *The Scottish Rite Ritual Monitor and Guide* by Arturo de Hoyos, 33°, and *A Bridge to Light* by Rex Hutchens, 33°, Grand Cross, as its textbooks, and is available at the low price of $35, plus s/h. [38]

The first required book, *The Scottish Rite Ritual Monitor and Guide*, edited by Arturo de Hoyos, is partly described on the official Scottish Rite Supreme Council web store[39] in these words:

---

38) www.scottishrite.org/about/masonic-education/srmc. Current as of 4/1/2011.
39) www.scottishritestore.org

A comprehensive guidebook to the Revised Standard Pike Ritual, the official ritual of the Supreme Council, this work contains more material than Albert Pike`s several Liturgies, as well as the complete texts of his Legendas and Readings in one handy volume.

Subjects include: Introductory material for new members, Albert Pike`s views on the nature and purposes of Freemasonry and the Scottish Rite in particular.

There can be no denying it. The *Ritual Monitor and Guide* in present use is largely Pike's work. And part of it clearly contains Pike's (and thus the Supreme Council's) "views on the nature and purpose of Freemasonry" as a whole, as well.

The second required book is *A Bridge to Light* by Rex Hutchens 33° (3rd edition, 2006), edited and introduced, once again, by Arturo de Hoyos. So it bears his stamp of authority, as well as that of the Supreme Council.

How does the book describe itself? You need go no further than the title page:

A BRIDGE TO LIGHT
The Revised Standard Pike Ritual

What could be more obvious? These leaders make it crystal clear where they stand on Pike, everywhere they turn. To put it another way, Pike's ritual and interpretations have stood the test of time within Scottish Rite Masonry for well over 130 years.

But now, let's take it a step further. Let's see what the most recent edition (2006) of that book, *A Bridge to Light*, says about Pike's *Morals and Dogma* and about his writings in general. First, let's look at the disclaimer:

> *A Bridge to Light* expresses the opinions of Dr. Rex R. Hutchens, 33°, GC, concerning the Scottish Rite Ritual and Albert Pike's *Morals and Dogma*. We respect his opinions and offer them for the consideration and personal evaluation of each reader of this volume.
>
> Similarly, *Morals and Dogma* represents the opinions of Albert Pike...

It may only represent the opinions of Rex Hutchens and Albert Pike, but look closer. The bottom of the page shows the entire leadership of the Scottish Rite, Southern Jurisdiction having or supporting the same "opinions:"

> This edition of *A Bridge to Light* conforms to the changes made in the Revised Standard Pike Ritual, which was adopted by this Supreme Council... [40]

---

40) The formal name for this "Supreme Council" is "The Supreme Council (Mother Council of the World) of the Inspectors General Knights Commander of the House of the Temple of Solomon of the Thirty-third and last degree of the Ancient and Accepted Scottish Rite of Freemasonry of the Southern Jurisdiction of the United States of America."

Let's add it up: Arturo de Hoyos, Masonic Grand Archivist and Grand Historian, approved and backed by the Supreme Council, Scottish Rite, Southern Jurisdiction, personally edited three important books:

1. *Esoterika: the Symbolism of the Blue Degrees of Freemasonry,* which was a previously unpublished work pertaining to all Masonry, by whom? Albert Pike.

2. *The Scottish Rite Ritual Monitor and Guide,* which is a revised version of what? The Standard *Pike* Ritual.

3. *A Bridge to Light: the Revised Standard Pike Ritual,* which is in addition an abbreviation and modern explanation of what? *Morals and Dogma,* written by whom? Albert Pike.

Read this carefully-crafted statement by Arturo de Hoyos:

Any discussion of Masonic government must start and end with one essential fact: all Masonic authority originates in a grand lodge. The Masonic Service Association of the United States (M.S.A.) has no authority over grand lodges. No Supreme Council, no respected author, nor any other group or person speaks for or controls Masonry; that prerogative rests solely with the grand lodges. Anyone doubting this need only check the cases when grand lodges have closed down the Scottish Rite, the Shrine, and other appendant Masonic bodies in their states or

suspended or expelled their "high officials."
It is a rare but powerful reminder of who is in
charge. [41]

While all that may be exactly true, it is pretty clear
that *A Bridge to Light* and these other books have stood
the test of time with the Masonic Lodge. That is why I
will use clear descriptions and statements from *A Bridge to
Light* almost exclusively in this book to answer the question, "Should a Christian be a Mason?"

So many authorities back Pike, whether simply "Blue
Lodge," Scottish Rite or York Rite that it seems clear that
the majority of Masons hold these general beliefs.

In this book I am not looking for off-the-wall, esoteric
beliefs. I am not looking for Satan underneath a rock. I
am specifically looking for those teachings that are easily and gladly taught to a Mason proceeding through the
degrees, in whatever body or appendant body he may be a
member.

What do those symbols mean? Where did they come
from? What do widely accepted authorities say they
mean? These are the main questions we will answer
throughout the rest of this book.

Following that will be one controversial topic: What
is the Baphomet? Is it ever mentioned in Masonry, and

---

41) Arturo de Hoyos and S Brent Morris, *Is It True What They Say about
Freemasonry?* 2nd edition, revised, (Silver Spring, MD: Masonic Information
Center, 1993, 1997). From Chapter 1, "The Methods of Anti-Masons."

are there clear, documented sources that reveal who or what the Baphomet really is? The answers to these questions will be right before your eyes.

So get out your King James (or Masonic King James) Bible and *A Bridge to Light* (if you have it), and follow along. You're about to see a side of Masonry that many people don't even notice. It's hiding in plain sight.

CHAPTER 4

◆

MASONRY'S POSITION ON THE BIBLE

Is the Bible Their Source and Guide?

In the last chapter you saw how Joseph Fort Newton was one of the few writers deemed worthy to write on "The Bible in Masonry," as I found in my friend's Masonic King James Bible. The publishers must have believed it to be very important.

You can find his works in various Masonic Grand Lodges, and at least one of his books is listed as recommended reading on many Grand Lodge websites.

One of his books, called *Brothers and Builders: the Basis and Spirit of Freemasonry,* has a very similar quote to the one in "The Bible in Masonry." But this quote tells much more than in the Masonic Bible, and it's much clearer, too. See for yourself below.

The following lengthy quote [42] contains so many important points. Let's read it a couple sentences at a

---

42) From *Brothers and Builders: the Basis and Spirit of Freemasonry* (1924), Chapter 2, "The Holy Bible." (All emphasis mine.)

time, so we may see clearly what this Masonic author claims is a basic belief of Masons:

> The fact that the Bible lies open upon its Altar means that man must have some Divine revelation —must seek for a light higher than human to guide and govern him. But Masonry lays down no hard and fast dogma on the subject of revelation. It attempts no detailed interpretation of the Bible.

Here Newton stated that man must have some kind of revelation from some kind of divinity, but what or who that is, is anyone's guess. And he says that Masonry doesn't try to interpret the Bible in detail. (So what does Masonry interpret about the Bible? We'll have to see.) Let's look at the next sentence:

> The great Book lies open upon its Altar, and is open for all to read, open for each to interpret for himself.

Isn't it funny that Newton says the "great Book" (the Bible) lies open for all to read? It's covered with those big compasses and square. If you're a Mason reading this, try to read a Bible with the big compasses and square sitting on it. I guarantee you, you can't read the Bible until you take off the stuff that's covering it.

> The tie by which our Craft is united is strong, but it allows the utmost liberty of faith and thought. It unites men, not upon a

> creed bristling with debated issues, but upon
> the broad, simple truth which underlies *all*
> creeds and over-arches all sects —faith in
> God, the wise Master Builder, for whom and
> with whom man must work.

So the Masons' Craft unites all creeds and *all* sects
with the simple truth that they should have faith in God?
The God of the Bible doesn't unite the devilish religions
of the world. What god do you think they are talking
about?

> Like everything else in Masonry, the Bible, so
> rich in symbolism, is itself a symbol —that
> is, a part taken for the whole. It is a symbol
> of the Book of Truth, the Scroll of Faith,
> the Record of the Will of God as man has
> learned it in the midst of the years— the per-
> petual revelation of Himself which God has
> made, and is making, to mankind in every
> age and land.

Let's pay attention to this "Great Masonic Divine's"
words. Joseph Fort Newton just said that in Masonry,
the Bible is not "the truth." The Bible is not "the Book
of Truth," either. It is merely "a symbol of the Book of
Truth." To them it is *a symbol* of a *nonexistent* book that
miraculously contains the combined wisdom of "every age
and land" that can claim one of the gods somewhere as
their own.

How can a Christian who believes the Bible also believe this lie that drops their Holy Bible down to the level of a second-rate symbol?

Does it *really* sound like the Bible is the "Great Light" of Masonry? It seems a lot more like the old bait-and-switch con. "Here, we'll take that old trusty Bible of yours and exchange it for a book that does not exist, that unites all theistic religions into one happy family!"

That does not sound very biblical.

The Bible to a Christian

God is perfectly clear about how His words are to be treated. Ironically, I can read it for myself in any King James Version Masonic Bible. In fact, I have a couple in front of me right now. The one I'm looking at is from the Lakewood [Ohio] Lodge No. 601, F&AM (Free and Accepted Masons) and is an exact duplicate of my friend's. Let's see what God says in this Masonic Bible.

First God spoke through Moses:

> Ye shall not add unto the word which I command you, neither shall ye diminish *ought* from it, that ye may keep the commandments of the LORD your God which I command you. [43]

If we add to or take away from God's words, we will

---

43) Deuteronomy 4:2. See also Deuteronomy 12:32.

never know which words are God's and which words are man's. How can we keep God's commandments if we don't know what they are? That is why God compiled His words in physical form as the Bible and preserved them through faithful followers to the present day.

Later, God spoke through Solomon as well:

> Every word of God is pure: he *is* a shield unto them that put their trust in him. Add thou not unto his words, lest he reprove thee, and thou be found a liar. [44]

We don't need to add to what God has already said. His words are different from any other words on earth. Every word of God is pure, and absolutely true, too, as God the Son, the Lord Jesus Christ stated:

> …If ye continue in my word, *then* are ye my disciples indeed; and ye shall know the truth, and the truth shall make you free. [45]

We can know the truth and be made free, by continuing to follow in Jesus' own word. And the Lord Jesus left no room for any other religion when He plainly stated:

> …I am the way, the truth, and the life: no man cometh unto the Father, but by me. [46]

The last thing we want is to be ashamed of Jesus' words. Jesus warned us:

44) Proverbs 30:5-6.
45) John 8:31-32.
46) John 14:6.

> Whosoever therefore shall be ashamed of me
> and of my words in this adulterous and sinful
> generation; of him also shall the Son of man
> be ashamed, when he cometh in the glory of
> his Father with the holy angels. [47]

Jesus clearly stated where the true "Great Light" is. Remember, this is a *promise* from the Lord and Saviour, Jesus Christ:

> ...I am the light of the world: he that fol-
> loweth me shall not walk in darkness, but
> shall have the light of life. [48]

So if we want the "light," we need go no further than follow the Lord Jesus Christ and His holy words, the Bible. Anyone who tells you something different is selling something.

In the next three chapters, let's find out about the "god" of Masonry.

---

47) Mark 8:38.
48) John 8:12.

♦ ———

CHAPTER 5

MASONIC SYMBOLS FOR DEITY

What Are the Sun and Moon in Masonry?

There are so many symbols used in Masonry that I had to limit the ones in this book to very few. But these will be enough to show you that according to their own approved writings, the god of Masonry is quite different from the One in the Bible.

The Triangle and the Eye: Sun and God

The flap is of sky blue with an open eye embroidered upon it in gold, denoting *the sun as the great archetype of light, the Ineffable Deity.* [49]

This quote says three things are the same: the sun, the archetype of light, [50] and the Ineffable [51] Deity.

So the symbol is of both the sun and God, sun-God. Did you also note the golden eye at the center of the sun? Are they trying to say something about their god? Let's look further.

The Eye of Gold: the Sun or the Deity

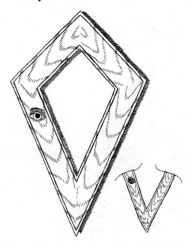

---

49) *A Bridge to Light,* pp. 14-15 (1995 edition, pp. 14-15), from "4th Degree: Secret Master." (Emphasis mine.)
50) This means when people think of light they think first of the sun. People get their symbols of light from the sun.
51) This means it is too overwhelming to a person to try and describe Deity.

The order[52] is a broad white watered ribbon worn as a collar. On the right side is painted an eye of gold, a symbol of the sun or of the Deity.[53]

So not only is the golden sun a symbol of Deity; so is the eye of gold you saw inside the sun. And here it is alone on the ribbon. You will be amazed how many Masonic symbols have multiple meanings, and how many of their symbols signify a god.

The Sun, Triangle and Star: God and "Correct Knowledge"

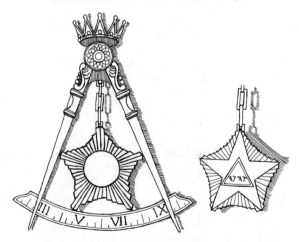

---

52) An order is a decoration indicating rank traditionally worn over the chest, whether a ribbon worn as a collar or a sash (as here), or an insignia pinned to a sash.

53) *A Bridge to Light*, 2006 edition, pp. 224-225, (1995 edition, pp. 246-247), from "27th Degree [1995 edition says 28th Degree]: Knight of the Sun or Prince Adept."

...Within the compasses is a medal, representing on one side the sun, and on the other a five-pointed star, in the center of which is a delta, and on that the name of Deity in Phoenician characters.... The sun as the source of light to our system was once worshiped as a god. The star as a type of the myriad suns that light other countless systems of worlds is an emblem of that Masonic Light in search of which every Mason travels —the correct knowledge of the Deity, and of His laws that control the universe. [54]

For some reason the author thought it was important to mention that the sun was once worshiped as a god. On the back of this "sun" is a five-pointed star with a triangle and the name of God in Phoenician letters.

Why is a symbol with God's name inside a five-pointed star? (You will find out in Chapter 7.)

The Sun and Moon: Also Osiris and Isis

The jewel is a heptagonal (seven-sided) medal, half gold and half silver or mother of pearl. These two colors are emblems of the sun and moon, themselves symbols of the Egyptian deities Osiris and Isis, ...

---

54) *A Bridge to Light*, 2006 edition, pp. 90-91, (1995 edition, pp. 94-95), from "14th Degree: Perfect Elu."

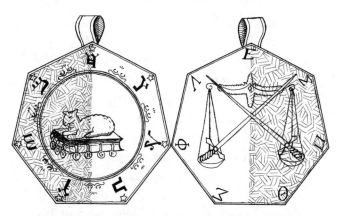

The Sun and Moon: Also Osiris and Isis

Let that sink in before we finish. The gold and silver represent the sun and moon, who are the Egyptian false gods Osiris and Isis. Now read the next part.

> Osiris and Isis... who represent the generative and productive powers of nature, illustrated in Masonic symbolism by the columns Jachin and Boaz as the active and passive forces manifested in nature (*Morals and Dogma*, p. 202). On one side are engraved, at the angles, the same letters as are on the capitals of the columns in the ceremony and possessing the same meaning, that of the last seven of the Sephiroth [55] of the Kabalah. [56]

---

55) Sephiroth are the 10 "divine attributes" of the impersonal Principle or deity, Ain-Soph in the book of Jewish mysticism, the Kabbalah.

56) *A Bridge to Light*, 2006 edition, pp. 124-125, (1995 edition, pp. 132-133), from "17th Degree: Knight of the East and West."

So gold and silver = the sun and moon = Osiris and Isis = the two columns, Jachin and Boaz = "the active and passive forces manifested in nature."

But this is not all. As you will see, the sun and moon have still more meanings, according to *A Bridge to Light.*

The Sun and Moon: Also Hermes/Mercury/ Thoth and the Master of the Lodge

The *frontispiece* for the Consistory Ritual shows an Egyptian figure with the words:

"Have you seen your Master today?"
"I have."
"How is he clothed?"
"In blue and gold."

"… the Egyptian Thoth is their equivalent of the Grecian Hermes and the Roman

Mercury, the true Grand Master of All Symbolic Lodges. From the earliest Masonic manuscripts we see Hermes represented as the ideal of the Master of the Lodge and in some traditions is even said to be the founder of Masonry. Pike, in his Second Lecture on Masonic Symbolism (p. 262) makes the following observation."

The "Master, clothed in blue and gold," of the Masons of a century and a half ago [1710], was Hermes; and Hermes and Mercury were the same. He is the "Master of the Lodge," associated with the Sun and Moon... [57]

So the "true Grand Master of All Symbolic Lodges," according to "the earliest Masonic manuscripts" is the false god Thoth, also called Hermes in Greek and Mercury in Latin. And who is this "Master of the Lodge" associated with? Once again, "the Sun and Moon." (Notice the capitalization of Sun and Moon.)

So the sun is seen in Masonry as:

- Deity.
- Once worshiped as a god.
- Represented in Masonry by a golden sun.
- Represented in Masonry by a golden eye.

---

57) *A Bridge to Light*, 2006 edition, p. 165 (1995 edition, pp. 174-175), from "20th Degree: Master of the Symbolic Lodge."

Together, the sun and moon are seen in Masonry as:

- The "Master of the Lodge."
- The false god Thoth, also known as Hermes or Mercury.
- The false gods Osiris and Isis.
- Represented in Masonry by gold and silver.
- Represented in Masonry by the columns Jachin and Boaz (originally in front of Solomon's Temple).
- Representing "the generative and productive powers of nature."
- Representing "the active and passive forces manifested in nature."

Does this sound *anything* like the God of the Bible? It sounds a whole lot like a fertility cult.

Let's go back to Osiris for a minute. It's just a symbol, right? You don't have to perform any rituals God hates, do you? Look for yourself.

Mourning the Sun

The candidate enters the Tabernacle in utter darkness and silence, a reminder of death. He hears the lamentations and sorrow associated with the deaths of selected deities—Osiris of Egypt, Kama of India, Mithra of Persia, Atys of Phrygia, and Thammuz of Phoenicia. Their deaths symbolize the temporary victory of darkness and evil over the light. The

> mythologies associated with all of these dei-
> ties tell of both their death and resurrection.
>
> Brethren, enacting ancient drama, mourn
> Osiris, who is representative of the sun, of
> light, of life, of good and of beauty. They
> reflect upon the way the earth may again
> be gladdened by his presence. Attempts are
> made to bring life to the dead Osiris with the
> grip of the Apprentice, a symbol of science,
> and with the grip of the Fellowcraft, a symbol
> of logic. [58]

So the candidate for the 24th Degree goes into a room
decorated with symbols, all designed to make him feel like
he entered into an ancient ceremony. In darkness he hears
men weeping for "the deaths of selected deities." Note
them again:

- Osiris (Egypt)
- Kama (India)
- Mithra (Persia)
- Atys (or Attis, Phrygia)
- Thammuz (or Tammuz or Dumuzi, Phoenicia and Babylon) [59]

These men are mourning for Osiris/Kama/Mithra/

58) *A Bridge to Light,* 2006 edition, p. 192 (1995 edition, pp. 204-205),
from "24th Degree: Prince of the Tabernacle."
59) Most of these false gods (and others) are discussed in *Babylon Religion:
How a Babylonian Goddess Became the Virgin Mary* (2006). Available from
Chick Publications.

Atys/Thammuz. Then they attempt using Masonic hand grips to raise this Osiris (etc.) from the dead. Doesn't this sound a lot like something God talked about in the Bible?

God showed this to the prophet Ezekiel in a vision:

> He said also unto me, Turn thee yet again, and thou shalt see greater abominations that they do. Then he brought me to the door of the gate of the LORD'S house which was toward the north; and, behold, there sat women *weeping* for Tammuz. [60]

According to God it is an *abomination* to weep for the death of Tammuz, or Osiris, Kama, Mithra or Attis, or any other false god. Whether as a candidate or a Mason participating in the ceremony, I would be doing exactly what these pagan women were doing. Should I, as a Christian, want to be part of a pagan ceremony that God completely condemns? You've got to be kidding.

We have talked about symbols Masons use for deity, whether about the true God or false gods. Now let's find out how Masonry views God the Son, Jesus Christ.

---

60) Ezekiel 8:13-14.

CHAPTER 6

◆

MASONIC TEACHINGS ABOUT JESUS

Is the Lord Jesus Christ like any other man? Absolutely not. Look at these scriptures about Jesus:

> God, who at sundry times and in divers manners spake in time past unto the fathers by the prophets, Hath in these last days spoken unto us by his Son, whom he hath appointed heir of all things, by whom also he made the worlds; [61]

God has spoken finally in His Son, more than any of His prophets. And by His Son all the worlds were made. That's pretty unique. Here's what God said through John:

> All things were made by him; and without him was not any thing made that was made. [62]

When Jesus asked His apostles who they say He was, God the Father gave Peter the answer:

> …Thou art the Christ, the Son of the living God. [63]

---

61) Hebrews 1:1-2.
62) John 1:3.
63) Matthew 16:16.

The Greek word *christos,* or "Christ" is the Hebrew word *mashiach,* or "Messiah." God the Father revealed to Peter that Jesus is *the* Messiah, *the* Son of *the* living God. Note what that means:

- Jesus is the Messiah—Jesus is the only Messiah. There was none before and there is none coming after, except for false Messiahs (false Christs). [64]

- Jesus is the Son—Jesus is the only begotten Son of the Father.

- There is only one living God—all other gods are false gods, or idols. [65]

Of a truth, there is only one God. All the others are false gods, idols of the people.

As the scriptures say:

> Tell ye, and bring them near; yea, let them take counsel together: who hath declared this from ancient time? who hath told it from that time? have not I the LORD? and *there is no God else beside me;* a just God and a Saviour; *there is none beside me.* [66]

And only through the one God can anyone be saved.

Look unto me, and be ye saved, all the ends

---

64) See Matthew 24:24 and Mark 13:22.
65) See 1 Chronicles 16:26 and Psalm 96:5.
66) Isaiah 45:21 (emphasis mine.) See also Deuteronomy 4:35, 39; 1 Samuel 2:2; 2 Samuel 7:22; 1 Kings 8:60; 1 Chronicles 17:20; Psalm 86:8; and Isaiah 45:6, 18, etc.

of the earth: for I am God, and *there is none
else.* [67]

So if Masonic writing drops Jesus down from being
the Messiah, the Son of the living God, into being just
another messiah, that is against the scriptures, isn't it?
Look for yourself. It's a lengthy quote, but very revealing:

> The purpose of teaching the concept of a
> Messiah in Freemasonry is to point out its
> near universality in the well-developed reli-
> gions of the ancient world. We see references
> to Dionysius of the Greeks, Sosiosch of the
> Persians, Krishna of the Hindus, Osiris of
> the Egyptians, Jesus of the Christians. The
> purpose of these varying cultures' messiahs
> was to find in human form a source of inter-
> cession with Deity; in particular one who, as
> a human, had been tempted and suffered the
> daily pangs of life and so could be expected
> to possess a particular sympathy and under-
> standing; in a word, the messiahs expressed
> hope. [68]

Look again. The author just pretended Jesus was the
same as:

- Dionysius of the Greeks.
- Sosiosch of the Persians.

---

67) Isaiah 45:22. (Emphasis mine.)
68) *A Bridge to Light*, 2006 edition, p. 106 (1995 edition, pp. 112-113),
from "Chapter of Rose Croix."

- Krishna of the Hindus.
- Osiris of the Egyptians.

What do these names have in common? Just one thing: they're all *false, pagan gods*. But the Lord Jesus Christ is the one and only true God and the way to heaven:

> Jesus saith unto him, I am the way, the truth, and the life: no man cometh unto the Father, but by me. [69]

Jesus lived in history. He died in history. He rose from the dead in history. Jesus is *not* a "mythological messiah."

Jesus is the only way to heaven. But in Masonry, He is made out to be simply one of the "ancients of the past," who gives us philosophical and religious instruction.

> In every degree, we are confronted with our duty directly or reminded of it via the opening and closing ritual or the characterization of such heroic figures as the Master Architect Hiram, King Solomon, Adoniram or Jacques De Molay. Duty forms the core of philosophical and religious instructions derived from the *ancients of the past:* Plato, Socrates, Pythagoras, Zoroaster, Jesus, Confucius. [70]

---

69) John 14:6.
70) *A Bridge to Light*, 2006 edition, pp. 16-17 (1995 edition, pp. 16-17), "4th Degree: Secret Master." (Emphasis mine.)

The author, Rex Hutchens, with the blessing of Arturo de Hoyos and the Supreme Council of the 33°, just tried to pass off the idea that the Creator of the universe and Son of God was not only one of many "messiahs," but also a mere equal to Plato, Socrates, Pythagoras, Zoroaster and Confucius.

These five are pagan philosophers. But look at the difference between them and our Lord Jesus Christ:

> ...our Lord Jesus Christ ...who is the blessed and *only* Potentate, the King of kings, and Lord of lords;[71]

> Looking for that blessed hope, and the glorious appearing of the great God and our Saviour Jesus Christ;[72]

Only a fool would equate our God, Saviour and Lord with some dead philosopher or a mythological character. I just cannot make the Jesus of Masonry square with the true Jesus of the Bible.

Now let's check out that five-pointed star symbol again. What is it *really* referring to?

---

71) 1 Timothy 6:14-15. See also Revelation 17:14 and 19:16.
72) Titus 2:13.

◆

CHAPTER 7

CHRIST IN A PENTAGRAM?

In Chapter 5 we saw a five-pointed star with a triangle and "the name of Deity" in Phoenician characters inside it. What was that about? Let's see if there are other clues between the pages of *A Bridge to Light*.

The Alpha-Omega Pentagram:
The Divine in the Human

It's hard to misinterpret what you are about to see and read.

Why is there an Alpha and Omega inside a pentagram? Let's let this foundational Masonic text speak for itself:

> These three lessons are symbolized by the pentagram or star with Alpha and Omega imposed on its surface. It is the symbol of the *Divine in man*. Alpha is the first letter of the Greek alphabet and Omega the last; hence, signifying completeness, the beginning and the end and all within them. The five-pointed star with a single point upward represents the Divine. It also symbolizes man for its five points allude to the five senses, the five members (head, arms and legs) and his five fingers on each hand, which signify the tokens that distinguish Masons. [73]

What did he say? There is a pentagram with Alpha and Omega, the symbol of Jesus, on it. Note this verse:

> I am Alpha and Omega, the beginning and the ending, saith the Lord, which is, and which was, and which is to come, the Almighty. [74]

Let's add up what this passage just said:

- The five-pointed star with a single point pointing upward represents the Divine.

---

73) *A Bridge to Light*, 2006 edition, pp. 192-193, (1995 edition, p. 205), from "24th Degree: Prince of the Tabernacle." (Emphasis mine.)
74) Revelation 1:8. See also Revelation 1:11; 21:6, 22:13.

- The same symbol also symbolizes man because of:
  - Five senses.
  - Five members (two arms, two legs, one head).
  - Five fingers on each hand (which are used by Masons to identify each other).

When the five-pointed star has Alpha and Omega, the symbol of Jesus, on it, it "is the symbol of the Divine in man."

If you are a Christian, you may not think that's such a bad thing. After all, the scripture clearly states:

> To whom God would make known what is the riches of the glory of this mystery among the Gentiles; which is *Christ in you,* the hope of glory:[75]

And:

> But ye are not in the flesh, but in the Spirit, if so be that the Spirit of God dwell in you. Now if any man have not the Spirit of Christ, he is none of his. And if *Christ be in you,* the body is dead because of sin; but the Spirit is life because of righteousness.[76]

And this:

> Examine yourselves, whether ye be in the faith; prove your own selves. Know ye not

75) Colossians 1:27.
76) Romans 8:9-10.

your own selves, how that *Jesus Christ is in you,* except ye be reprobates?[77]

All that is true. Jesus Christ, the Spirit of Christ, *is* in Christians. But is He in *all* Masons? And doesn't a pentagram have other meanings? Let's look at more references.

The Pentagram as Ahura and the Four Male Emanations

The five-pointed Star, with all its lines united, represents *Ahura* and the four male Emanations, and every cross represents these four.[78]

So who or what is Ahura? *A Bridge to Light explains:*

Ahura Mazda, said the early Persians, is the

---

77) 2 Corinthians 13:5.
78) *A Bridge to Light*, 2006 edition, p. 305, (1995 edition, p. 318), from "32nd Degree: Master of the Royal Secret."

Creator and Author of all things. In Him abides the intellect which reveals itself in the universe as action and in men as human intellect. Existing within *Ahura Mazda* are *Spenta Mainyu* and *Vohumano*, the source of life, light and the pure intellect.

The ancient Sabaens of eastern Arabia recognized *Mithra* as the Grand Artificer of the universe, the Spirit of the sun and Light and the Eye of *Ahura Mazda.* He is three in one for his essence illuminates, warms and makes fruitful.[79]

What are those "four male Emanations" that every cross in the pentagram represents? From the same chapter:

- Spenta Mainyu
- Vohu-Mano
- Asha
- Khshathra[80]

Ahura is not another name for Jesus. It is one of the many names of the god Tammuz, when he is depicted as a winged globe.[81] And here he is the chief deity in the Zoroastrian religion, *Ahura Mazda,* known as *Ormazd* to the Greeks.

As I told you, the same symbol actually means many things in Masonry, and it's revealed only in degrees. The

79) *A Bridge to Light*, 2006 edition, p. 216, (1995 edition, pp. 230-231), from "26th Degree: Prince of Mercy." (Emphasis mine.)
80) *A Bridge to Light*, 2006 edition, p. 303, (1995 edition, p. 316), from "32nd Degree: Master of the Royal Secret."
81) See Daniels, *Babylon Religion*, (2006), p. 89 footnote 1, and p. 98.

Alpha-Omega-pentagram was in the 24th Degree, and the Ahura connection here was revealed in the 32nd Degree.

So when it says "Divine" in Masonry, it is impossible for a Christian to tell which god it's referring to. So you can't just "pick and choose" which god or gods you like and which you don't. It's a package deal that you are stuck with. Like it or not, you have to do some kind of homage to a whole bunch of pagan deities, even if you try only to look for the "Christian symbols."

Let's examine one more quote on "the Divine in man." This one is found in the 25th Degree:

> In the House of the Planets, the soul is the principle concern; we learn *the soul of man is a part of the Divine.* In the House of the Sun and Moon we learn that within man is the *divine Intelligence.* The threefold nature of man— his flesh, his soul and his intellect— combine to form the human. When cultivated properly, the voice of God may be heard in the human mind and heart. [82]

There are three points to this paragraph:

1. The soul of man is a part of the Divine —not a creation of God— an actual part of Him!

2. Within man is the divine Intelligence.

---

82) *A Bridge to Light*, 2006 edition, p. 205, (1995 edition, p. 220), from "25th Degree: Knight of the Brazen Serpent." (Emphasis mine.)

3. Man can cultivate his mind and heart to hear the voice of God.

Does the Bible agree? Let's see. First, man's soul was *created by God,* [83] it's not a part of Him:

> And so it is written, The first man Adam *was made a living soul...* [84]

Second, *no* good thing dwells within man:

> For I know that in me (that is, in my flesh,) dwelleth *no good thing:* for to will is present with me; but how to perform that which is good I find not. [85]

Third, the heart cannot be "cultivated" to hear God. It is desperately wicked:

> The heart is deceitful above all things, and desperately wicked: who can know it? [86]

None of this is Christian. It is clearly non-Christian, even anti-Christian. How can a Christian believe all these pagan doctrines we keep finding in plain sight?

Now it is time to answer these final questions: Who or what is the spirit behind Masonry, and what is this "Baphomet" that people claim Masons worship?

---

83) 1 Corinthians 15:45. See also Genesis 2:7.
84) 1 Corinthians 15:45.
85) Romans 7:18.
86) Jeremiah 17:9.

CHAPTER 8

◆

BAPHOMET: MASONRY'S DIRTY SECRET

If you read books or hear discussions of Masonry, sooner or later you will hear the term *Baphomet*. Masons will deny any connection with the strange image. But you are about to see that Albert Pike knew what the Baphomet was, and wrote about it in *Morals and Dogma*.

Furthermore, you will see the undeniable connections between Pike and the French occultist Éliphas Lévi, as well as additional information on the Baphomet that Pike did not dare to reveal.

Éliphas Lévi's Influence on Masonry

"Éliphas Lévi Zahed" was not his birth name. Instead, it was the result of him trying to turn his real name, "Alphonse Louis Constant," into Hebrew. But "Éliphas Lévi" (1810-1875) was not Jewish.

He was a French shoemaker's son who went to seminary in Paris to become a Roman Catholic priest. Eventually he was kicked out for teaching doctrines contrary to the Catholic religion. Still later he committed the ultimate crime for a Catholic seminarian: he fell in love with a woman. That ended his priestly ambitions.

Instead, he became interested in Rosicrucianism and other forms of the occult. Starting in 1855, Lévi published a number of books in French, which were later translated into English by occultist and mystic Arthur Edward Waite (1857-1942).

Éliphas Lévi

A number of occultic books by Lévi in the original French ended up in the library of none other than Albert Pike (1809-1891). Did they influence him? You bet they did. This is freely admitted by Masons:

> In the library left by Albert Pike are a number of books on the occult, by "Éliphas Levi"

(Alphonse Louis Constant), which in the [eighteen] seventies were not [yet] translated into English. Levi was, perhaps, the greatest of French mystics and Cabalists. General Pike borrowed considerably from Levi in his degrees of "Knight of the Sun" and "Prince of the Royal Secret."[87]

Anytime someone talks about the Baphomet, he is usually talking about the writings of Lévi. But Lévi also drew the most famous image of it, used by occultists and Satanists to this very day. Here is the Baphomet, exactly as Lévi drew it[88] (for which I apologize in advance).

87) From "Albert Pike, Mystic" by Henry R. Evans, Litt D in *The Master Mason*, May 1925. Online at www.themasonictrowel.com.
88) Éliphas Lévi, *Transcendental Magic: Its Doctrine and Ritual: A Complete Translation of "Dogme et Rituel de la Haute Magie"* (1855-56) with a Biographical Preface; translated by Arthur Edward Waite (London: George Redway, 1896), p. 174.

Descriptions of the Baphomet

Did you notice one familiar item on the Baphomet? I've blown it up to make it clear:

That's the same pentagram as those in *A Bridge to Light*.

Do you think this is all a coincidence? Think again.

How Albert Pike described the Baphomet

Let's take a look at an amazing statement about the Baphomet, first made by occultist Éliphas Lévi. Then we'll quote a very similar statement by... who else? Albert Pike. It's long, but trust me, it's worth it.

Éliphas Lévi in *The Mysteries of Magic:* [89]

THERE exists a force in Nature which is far more powerful than steam, and by whose means a single man, who can master it and knows how to direct it, might throw the world into confusion and transform its face.

This force was known to the ancients; it consists of a universal agent whose supreme law is equilibrium, and whose direction depends immediately on the Great Arcanum of transcendent magic.

By the direction of this agent we can change the very order of the seasons, produce in the night the phenomena of day, correspond instantaneously from one end of the earth to the other, discern, like Apollonius, what is taking place at the Antipodes, heal or hurt at a distance, and endow human speech with a universal reverberation and success. This agent, which barely manifests under the uncertainties of the art of Mesmer and his followers, is precisely what the mediaeval adepts called the first matter of the *magnum opus.*

The Gnostics made it the burning body of

89 *The Mysteries of Magic: A Digest of the Writings of Éliphas* Lévi, translated by Arthur Edward Waite (London: George Redway, 1886), "The Great Magic Agent, or the Mysteries of the Astral Light," pp. 74-75. See also Éliphas Lévi, *Transcendental Magic: Its Doctrine and Ritual,* translated by Arthur Edward Waite (London: George Redway, 1896), pp. 13-14. (Emphasis mine.)

the Holy Ghost, and this it was which was adored in the secret rites of the Sabbath or the Temple under the symbolic figure of Baphomet, or of the Androgyne Goat of Mendes.

This ambiant *[sic]* and all-penetrating fluid, this ray detached from the sun's splendour, and fixed by the weight of the atmosphere and by the power of central attraction, this body of the Holy Ghost, which we call the Astral Light and the Universal Agent, this electro-magnetic ether, this vital and luminous caloric is represented on ancient monuments by the girdle of Isis, which twines in a love-knot round two poles, by the bull-headed serpent, by the serpent with the head of a goat or dog, in the ancient theogonies, and by the serpent devouring its own tail..."

Now here is a very similar quote from Albert Pike in *Morals and Dogma:*[90]

[Identical translations of the French are in **bold text.** Similar translations are <u>underlined</u>. All other words are Pike's own words.]

> **There** <u>is</u> **in nature** <u>one most potent</u> **force, by means** <u>whereof</u> **a single man, who** <u>could possess himself of</u> **it,** <u>and should know</u> **how**

---

90 *Morals and Dogma* (1871-present), p. 734. (Emphasis mine.)

to direct it, could revolutionize and change the face of the world. This force was known to the ancients.

It is a universal agent, whose Supreme law is equilibrium; and whereby, if science can but learn how to control it, it will be possible to change the order of the Seasons, to produce in night the phenomena of day, to send a thought in an instant round the world, to heal or slay at a distance, to give our words universal success, and make them reverberate everywhere.

This agent, partially revealed by the blind guesses of the disciples of Mesmer, is precisely what the Adepts of the middle ages called the elementary matter of the great work.

The Gnostics held that it composed the igneous body of the Holy Spirit; and it was adored in the secret rites of the Sabbat or the Temple, under the hieroglyphic figure of Baphomet or the hermaphroditic goat of Mendes.

There is a Life-Principle of the world, a universal agent, wherein are two natures and a double current, of love and wrath.

This ambient fluid penetrates everything. It is a ray detached from the glory of the Sun,

and fixed by the weight of the atmosphere and the central attraction.

<u>It is the</u> **body of the Holy** <u>Spirit</u>, **the universal Agent, the Serpent devouring** <u>his</u> **own tail**. With **this electro-magnetic ether, this vital and luminous caloric**, the <u>ancients</u> and the alchemists were familiar."

Wow! Albert Pike just quoted or translated differently almost 3/4 of occultist Éliphas Lévi's words. And taking into account that both Waite and Pike individually translated Lévi's words from the original French (no English was yet available), the picture becomes clear. Pike didn't just reference Éliphas Lévi and quote him. Pike *identified* with him, *believed* his ideas, *stole his words*, slightly modified them and made them his own.

Let's summarize: Lévi and Pike both said the Baphomet had a number of other identities. Note these especially:

- The burning (igneous) body of the Holy Ghost.
- The androgyne (male & female) Goat of Mendes.
- The serpent devouring its own tail.

The serpent devouring its own tail

Both Pike and Lévi said that the Baphomet is also represented by a serpent devouring its own tail. Does that mean the snake in the image below from the seal of Solomon in *A Bridge to Light* is the Baphomet as well?

THE GREAT SYMBOL OF SOLOMON

Yes, that snake you see encircling the "seal of Solomon," biting its tail, is another symbol of the Baphomet.[91]

This picture is in *A Bridge to Light* in the "Knight of the Sun" Degree. But where did it come from? Not from Pike's *Morals and Dogma*, but from Éliphas Lévi's *Transcendental Magic: Its Doctrine and Ritual* (p. 2). So even the modern book *A Bridge to Light* borrowed from the occultist Éliphas Lévi. I doubt those authors were ignorant of Lévi's occultic writings, either.

What's missing from Pike's quotation of Lévi

Did you notice that Pike finished the last paragraph in the quotation above by going in a different direction?

---

91) It is also called "...the Gnostic worm ouroboros, which is a simplified dragon or serpent biting its tail..." See *A Bridge to Light*, 2006 edition, pp. 227-228 (1995 edition, pp. 251-252), from "The 27th Degree: Knight of the Sun, or Prince Adept" (1995 edition says 28th Degree).

He didn't dare put the rest of Lévi's words into *Morals and Dogma*. Want to know what they were?

Here is *what's missing* after "the serpent devouring its own tail," in Pike's quote of Lévi:

> ...emblem of prudence and of Saturn. It is the winged dragon of Medea, the double serpent of the caduceus, and *the tempter of Genesis;* but it is also the brazen snake of Moses, encircling the Tau, that is, the generative lingam; it is the Hyle of the Gnostics, and the double tail which forms the legs of the solar cock of Abraxos. Lastly, it is *the devil of exoteric dogmatism,* and is really *the blind force which souls must conquer,* in order to detach themselves from the chains of earth; for if their will should not free them from its fatal attraction, they will be absorbed in the current by the same power which first produced them, and will return to the central and eternal fire.

Wait a second. This is saying that the Baphomet is not only the snake biting its tail, a blind force, and the "burning body of the Holy Ghost," but it's also "the tempter of Genesis"... and something called "the devil of exoteric dogmatism." Is this referring to the Devil himself? Let's see.

There is no doubt that Pike called the Baphomet

"the igneous (burning) body of the Holy Spirit." Pike also called the Baphomet simply "the body of the Holy Spirit," But if he also believed it to be the Devil, this would be blasphemy against the Holy Ghost. You cannot label God the Holy Ghost as the Devil.

Could the "Holy Ghost" of the Masons be the Devil?

Maybe I misunderstood. When I read this, I was dumbfounded. But I needed confirmation, so I checked a book that Pike owned, translated and quoted approvingly—Lévi's *Transcendental Magic*—for any other clues. Wait till you see what I found.

There were numerous references to the Baphomet, but this one was clearest.

> We return once more to that terrible number fifteen, *symbolized in the Tarot* by a monster throned upon an altar, mitred and horned, having a woman's breasts and the generative organs of a man, a chimera, a malformed sphinx, a synthesis of monstrosities; below this figure we read a frank and simple inscription—THE DEVIL.[92]

The Tarot is a special deck of cards that is used in divination (fortune-telling). All forms of divination are

---

92) *Transcendental Magic: Its Doctrine and Ritual,* translated by Arthur Edward Waite (London: George Redway, 1896), Chapter XV, "The Sabbath of the Sorcerers," pp. 288-289. (Emphasis mine.)

forbidden by God.[93] Card number 15 mentioned above is "the Devil" card. And what figure is on that card? You have already seen it. Here is another version from the later Rider-Waite-Smith Tarot deck:

This is card 15 from the Rider-Waite-Smith Tarot deck.[94] That "Waite" is none other than Arthur Edward Waite, the translator of French occultist Éliphas Lévi's books.

Now it is undeniably clear. That unmistakable figure of the Baphomet (though a little different from Lévi's original illustration) is the Devil. In case it was not obvious enough, Lévi clarified:

> Yes, we confront here *the phantom of all terrors, the dragon* of all theogonies, the Ariman of the Persians, the Typhon of the Egyptians, the Python of the Greeks, *the old serpent of the Hebrews,* the fantastic monster, the nightmare, the Croquemitaine, the gargoyle, the great beast of the middle ages, and, worse than all this, *the Baphomet of the Templars,* the bearded idol of the alchemists, *the obscene deity of Mendes, the goat of the Sabbath.* The frontispiece to this Ritual reproduces the exact figure of the terrible emperor of night, with all his attributes and all his characters.

But Lévi did not stop at blaspheming the Holy Ghost by calling Him the serpent of Genesis, Baphomet and the Devil. Lévi continued:

> Let us state now for the edification of the vulgar…for the greater glory of the Church, which persecuted Templars, burnt magicians, excommunicated Freemasons, &c. let us state boldly and precisely that all the inferior initiates of the occult sciences and profaners of the great arcanum, not only did in the past, but do now, and will ever, adore what is signified by this alarming symbol.

Everyone knows that the Baphomet is not an actual

living, breathing creature. It is a *symbol*. But Lévi is now revealing of what it is the symbol. And Lévi just confessed that all the past, present and future "inferior initiates" (meaning, all those in lower levels) "of the occultic sciences" adore (worship) what is signified by the Baphomet, which he has confessed is actually the Devil.

So is Lévi saying that occultists of all kinds really worship the Devil? You just read it for yourself.

Not only that, but did you notice *who* Lévi named as being the "inferior initiates of the occult sciences" in that quote? The previous sentence listed Templars, magicians ... *and Freemasons*. So as you have seen in many other places, it is both admitted and presumed that those entering Masonry are actually being initiated into the occult. Then Lévi wrote:

> Yes, in our profound conviction, the Grand Masters of the Order of the Templars *worshipped the Baphomet, and caused it to be worshipped by their adepts;* yes, there existed in the past, and there may be still in the present, assemblies which are presided over by this figure, seated on a throne and having a flaming torch between the horns; but the adorers of this sign do not consider, as do we, that *it is the representation of the devil;* on the contrary, for them it is that of the god Pan, the god of our modern schools of philosophy,

the god of the Alexandrian theurgic school, and of our own mystical Neoplatonists, the god of Lamartine and Victor Cousin, the god of Spinoza and Plato, the god of the primitive Gnostic schools; *the Christ* also of the dissident priesthood; this last qualification, ascribed to *the goat of black magic*, will not astonish students of religious antiquities who are acquainted with the phases of symbolism and doctrine in their various transformations, whether in India, Egypt, or Judea.

So Lévi stated that people who worship the Baphomet, "the goat of black magic," are really worshipping Jesus Christ? This is from the writings Albert Pike quoted approvingly in *Morals and Dogma*?

That's it. What more could Éliphas Lévi (or Albert Pike) do, to do "despite unto the Spirit of grace"?[95]

He has taken the perverted androgynous goat-headed monster Baphomet, and claimed it was "the burning body of the Holy Ghost," then the Devil himself, and then Christ! (If you are in doubt, read that last sentence of the quote again slowly, out loud to yourself.)

When you claim the Devil is Christ and the body of Holy Ghost, you have committed blasphemy against Christ and the Holy Ghost. The Lord Jesus Christ was very clear about what blasphemies can be forgiven:

---

95) See Hebrews 10:29.

> And whosoever shall speak a word against
> the Son of man, it shall be forgiven him: but
> unto him that blasphemeth against the Holy
> Ghost it shall not be forgiven. [96]

That is one thing I *never* want to do. So why would anyone dare risk falling into such condemnation by submitting to higher and higher degrees of Masonic service?

"But these are only symbols," one may protest. "Even the quote from Lévi showed that people saw other things *behind* the symbols, that were not as bad as that picture of Baphomet. Pike was one of those people. He didn't believe Baphomet was the Devil. That's why he didn't quote the rest of Lévi," some may rationalize.

Then what *did* Pike believe? Do you see the problem when you try to interpret symbols that mean something different at different degrees and under different circumstances?

The pentagram is just one example. The Baphomet is a bigger one. When can you say to yourself, "Now I *know* the meaning of the Baphomet"? The deception just keeps getting wider and bigger.

Pike actually mentioned the Baphomet one more time on page 818 of *Morals and Dogma*. Please notice his use of the word "adepts." [97] I will break down the passage; but

---

96) Luke 12:10. See also Mark 3:28-29.
97) A mysterious Mason who is beyond even the "High Degrees" of the Craft.

you tell me whether Pike is being forthcoming with what he really believes.

Pike's second Baphomet quote [98]

It is absurd to suppose that men of intellect adored a monstrous idol called Baphomet, or recognized Mahomet as an inspired prophet. Their symbolism, invented ages before, to conceal what it was dangerous to avow, was of course misunderstood by those who were not adepts, and to their enemies seemed to be pantheistic. The calf of gold, made by Aaron for the Israelites, was but one of the oxen under the laver of bronze, and the Karobim on the Propitiatory, misunderstood.

Pike is trying to persuade us that the golden calf that people committed idolatry with was actually one of the oxen under the laver of bronze in front of the Tabernacle, and that the angelic Cherubim in the holy of holies over the ark of the covenant was actually a calf as well, not an angel. This doesn't even make sense.

Moses hadn't come down from the mount yet to show the temple designs, so they didn't even know about the oxen or the cherubim. Pike's words are completely false. Let this be a lesson to us all: read Pike, and all Masonic materials, slowly and *very carefully!*

---

98) See *Morals and Dogma*, pp. 818-819, "30ᵗʰ Degree: Knight Kadosh."

> The symbols of the wise always become
> the idols of the ignorant multitude. What
> the Chiefs of the Order really believed and
> taught, is indicated to the Adepts by the
> hints contained in the high Degrees of Free-
> Masonry, and by the symbols which only the
> Adepts understand.

So Pike said the *true* beliefs and teachings of Masonry are only *hinted at* in the high degrees of Masonry. This means that in the lower degrees they don't even come close to what the Chiefs of the Order truly believe. If they only "hint" in the higher degrees, how long will it be before they (whoever "they" are) stop "hinting" and say what they truly believe?

> The Blue Degrees are but the outer court or
> portico of the Temple. Part of the symbols
> are displayed there to the Initiate, but he is
> intentionally misled by false interpretations.
> It is not intended that he shall understand
> them; but it is intended that he shall imagine
> he understands them.

Thanks. So a guy joins an order, and is continually and *intentionally* "misled by false interpretations." That seems pretty plain to me. Those first three "Blue Degrees" are *intended to mislead.* They want people to think they understand them, but they don't. Should a Christian join an organization that continually lies to him like that?

Their true explication [99] is reserved for the
Adepts, the Princes of Masonry. The whole
body of the Royal and Sacerdotal Art was
hidden so carefully, centuries since, in the
High Degrees, as that it is even yet impossible to solve many of the enigmas which they
contain.

So the so-called "Adepts," the "Princes of Masonry,"
whoever they are (and Pike never tells who they are) hid
Masonry's "Royal and Sacerdotal [100] Art" "so carefully"
that even people in the 30th, 31st, 32nd and 33rd Degrees
would find it impossible even in the present day to solve
the enigmas (mysteries) in the Masonic society.

Isn't it strange? This sounds a lot like that famous
quote about Lucifer being the god of Masonry that some
attribute to Pike. But I'm not reading disputed words of a
private speech in an old French publication. I am simply
quoting *Morals and Dogma*, a book you can view online
or in any Masonic lodge.

Look what Pike said next:

It is well enough for the mass of those called
Masons, to imagine that all is contained in
the Blue Degrees; and whoso attempts to
undeceive them will labor in vain, and without any true reward violate his obligations as

---

99) Explication is making the meaning clear.
100) Sacerdotal refers to the authority of priests.

an Adept. Masonry is the veritable Sphinx,
buried to the head in the sands heaped round
it by the ages.

Pike here bragged that even if an Adept were to violate his Masonic oaths and obligations to keep Masonry secret, then leave Masonry, he would "labor in vain" to try and "un-deceive" the Masons in the first three Blue Degrees. They will not believe even an Adept, because they still will think they understand Masonry. But they are completely deceived.

How did they pull this off? According to Pike, Masonry is as buried in layers of secrets as the Sphinx was buried to the head in centuries of sands in Egypt.

How can anyone other than the most advanced Mason *ever* claim to understand Masonry? And how can a Christian say, "As a Mason, I will never violate my Christian faith," if he has no idea what *is* true Masonry?

I end here with a clear admission in plain sight, in the Introduction to the 2006 edition of *A Bridge to Light:*

...Whatever the truth of history, the contributions to the symbolism of Freemasonry by the religion, philosophies, mythologies and occult mysteries of the past lie upon its surface for all to see. [101]

Ironically, as you have seen, he's telling the truth. All

---

101) *A Bridge to Light* (2006), p. 1.

the "religion, philosophies, mythologies and occult mysteries" are in plain sight. But then the author states:

> Rather than being a secret society, Freemasonry
> is a revealer of secrets.

Are you kidding? Freemasonry wraps *everything* in secrets.

- Where did Masonry really come from?
- What do Masons really believe?
- Who do Masons really worship?
- Who really runs Masonry?

Those are questions they refuse to answer. But you have just seen the facts laid bare from their own accepted writings. You have also seen their blasphemies about the Father, Son and Holy Ghost, and causing the Mason to commit idolatrous abominations (remember the weeping for Tammuz?). This is why no Christian should *ever* become a Mason. And any Christian who is a Mason should get out immediately.

> Be not deceived; God is not mocked: for
> whatsoever a man soweth, that shall he also
> reap. [102]

You need to decide what you want to sow, and be ready to give account for it before God. [103]

---

102) Galatians 6:7.
103) See Romans 14:12 and Hebrews 9:27.

CHAPTER 9

———— ◆ ————

CONCLUSION

I started this book by exposing the origins and foundational beliefs of Masonry, to begin answering the question, "Should a Christian be a Mason?"

In order to fully answer that question, we needed to know who to trust for information on Masonry. Time and again, in Masonic Bibles and from Masonic scholars, the answer came: Albert Pike.

- One of my Masonic Bibles describes the Blue Degrees, and both the York and Scottish Rite appendant bodies, by quoting Pike.

- Major Masonic leaders have cited Pike.

- The Scottish Rite has based its teachings, rituals and symbols and their meanings on Pike's works.

- One of the two main books pushed for anyone reaching the 3rd Degree and wanting to know about the Scottish Rite, is *A Bridge to Light*, a summary and explanation of Albert Pike's *Morals and Dogma*.

Yes, Arturo de Hoyos explained that the Grand Lodge of any state or jurisdiction can decide what is allowed within Masonry. But the plain fact is, for 140 years Pike's teachings have been passed down, largely unchanged and unchallenged. When *A Bridge to Light* points the reader to a book to further explain any doctrine, it points unfailingly to Pike's *Morals and Dogma*.

So I was able to confidently spend most of the rest of the book quoting *A Bridge to Light* in showing the pagan mythologies, pagan rituals and pagan philosophies that fill the Degrees of Masonry, especially in the Scottish Rite, but with ancient symbolism found in all Masonic bodies.

And I barely scratched the surface. You only saw symbols, images and rituals that directly concerned God, God the Son (Jesus Christ) and God the Holy Ghost. I ignored many more doctrines and rituals in order to focus on these facts and keep the size of the book small.

Then with some hesitation, I prayed and was convicted that I needed to cover the Baphomet that many people say is behind Masonry. What I found astounded me. Not only did Albert Pike say that somehow a powerful force was both "the igneous body of the Holy Spirit" and the obscene Baphomet, the goat of Mendes.

He also translated a famous passage in *Morals and Dogma* about the Baphomet from a well-known French occultist named Éliphas Lévi. That meant that Pike read Lévi and knew what he left out of his quote. Pike knew that Lévi taught that the Baphomet-body of the Holy Spirit was also the Devil.

That led me to find more of Lévi's writings and confirm what I had read. And in them I found an extra fact: that he also equated Baphomet to our Lord and Saviour, Jesus Christ. No reasonable person, no matter how newly a Christian, could equate Jesus Christ to the Devil, even with the most cursory reading of the Gospels. This is blasphemy, pure and simple.

That also means that equating what Lévi called both Baphomet and the Holy Ghost with the Devil was also blasphemy. It's hard not to call it what it is: blasphemy against the Holy Ghost.

So I am led to make a very clear statement: no Christian should ever be a Mason. And any Christian who is a Mason should get out immediately.

We must choose the one or the other!

God spoke directly to this through the apostle Paul:

> And have no fellowship with the unfruitful works of darkness, but rather reprove *them*. For it is a shame even to speak of those things which are done of them in secret. [104]

If you are a Christian who is into Masonry, ask yourself: "Which will I choose?" Look at these scriptures. You need to decide which is more important to you: Christ or Masonry.

And if it seem evil unto you to serve the

---

104) Ephesians 5:11-12.

LORD, *choose you this day whom ye will serve*; whether the gods which your fathers served that *were* on the other side of the flood, or the gods of the Amorites, in whose land ye dwell: but as for me and my house, we will serve the LORD. [105]

No man can serve two masters: for either he will hate the one, and love the other; or else he will hold to the one, and despise the other. Ye cannot serve God and mammon. [106]

But *I say*, that the things which the Gentiles sacrifice, they sacrifice to devils, and not to God: and *I would not that ye should have fellowship with devils.* [107]

If you have not done so, check all these references yourself. Aside from the readings of *A Bridge to Light*, they are mostly accessible on the internet at www.books. google.com, or at www.archive.org. I want you to understand what is at stake, and my prayer is that you make the right decision, one that you can defend before Almighty God on Judgment Day.

God bless you as you make the right choice.

---

105) Joshua 24:15.
106) Matthew 6:24. See also Luke 16:13.
107) 1 Corinthians 10:20.

CHAPTER 10

◆

NOW WHAT DO I DO?

If you have decided to leave Masonry, you are doing the right thing. Right now you need to pray to God and ask for His forgiveness for your involvement in Masonry.

You may pray to Him something like this:

> Father in heaven, thank You for showing me what You think about Masonry. I now reject its unbiblical, sinful and blasphemous practices. Please forgive me for my fellowship with the unfruitful works of darkness. I trust the Lord Jesus as the only Light of the world and my only Saviour. Thank You, Father, in Jesus' name, amen.

If you have not done so, you need to spend your time more wisely, "redeeming the time, because the days are evil." [108] Find a church where the Lord Jesus Christ is preached, and the Bible is the final authority. If possible, find one that does not have any Masons in positions of authority. They will not have power over you, but they may tempt you to fall back into your old lifestyle.

PASTOR KEVIN
(509) 697-7833

---

108) Ephesians 5:16; Colossians 4:5.

If you don't have one, get yourself a King James Bible that does not have all those Masonic notes in it. Praying and reading the scriptures is very important for you to have a godly life. Look at 2 Timothy 3:16-17:

> All scripture is given by inspiration of God, and is profitable for doctrine, for reproof, for correction, for instruction in righteousness: That the man of God may be perfect, throughly furnished unto all good works.

And:

> According as his divine power hath given unto us all things that pertain unto life and godliness, through the knowledge of him that hath called us to glory and virtue: Whereby are given unto us exceeding great and precious promises: that by these ye might be partakers of the divine nature, having escaped the corruption that is in the world through lust. (2 Peter 1:3-4)

You want your life to reflect the qualities God expects in Christian leaders, as found in 1 Timothy 3:2-9:

> 2 A bishop then must be blameless, the husband of one wife, vigilant, sober, of good behaviour, given to hospitality, apt to teach;

> 3 Not given to wine, no striker, not greedy of filthy lucre; but patient, not a brawler, not covetous;

4 One that ruleth well his own house, having his children in subjection with all gravity;

5 (For if a man know not how to rule his own house, how shall he take care of the church of God?)

6 Not a novice, lest being lifted up with pride he fall into the condemnation of the devil.

7 Moreover he must have a good report of them which are without; lest he fall into reproach and the snare of the devil.

8 Likewise must the deacons be grave, not doubletongued, not given to much wine, not greedy of filthy lucre;

9 Holding the mystery of the faith in a pure conscience.

These are not just ideals for church leaders. These are God's desire for you as a Christian, as well. Find godly people to spend your time with. But don't forsake spending time with your family, if you have one. Proverbs 27:17 says:

Iron sharpeneth iron; so a man sharpeneth the countenance of his friend.

Find godly counselors who will assist you on your Christian spiritual journey. God's word says:

A wise man is strong; yea, a man of knowledge increaseth strength. For by wise counsel

thou shalt make thy war: and in multitude of
counsellors there is safety. (Proverbs 24:5-6)

You are leaving an ungodly use of your time. You
need to replace that with spending your time in a way
God approves. Over time, Jesus will heal your wounds
and start to make you the person that He wants you to
be. And your family and friends will see the difference. As
the scripture says:

Let your light so shine before men, that they
may see your good works, and glorify your
Father which is in heaven. (Matthew 5:16)

May the Lord bless you and lead you into a godly
Christian fellowship and lifestyle.

If You Decided NOT to Leave Masonry

If you have decided NOT to leave Masonry, I have
one question for you.

Why?

Why would you refuse to leave an organization that
goes against your Christian beliefs, clearly contradicts the
Bible, lifts up false gods and lowers Jesus Christ to the
level of pagan philosophers and His gospel to a myth?

Why would you seek "light" in Masonry, when Jesus
is already the light of the world, and His followers walk in
His light, not in darkness (John 8:12)?

Look honestly into your heart. Think about the awesome sacrifice Jesus Christ made for you. Do you really want to grieve the holy Spirit of God that has sealed you unto the day of redemption (Ephesians 4:30)? Is it...

- peer pressure?
- a desire to belong?
- living up to family tradition?
- do you want to get ahead in business?
- do you desire to climb the ladder to higher degrees?

Be honest with yourself before God. When you know why you want to remain a Mason, see if you can pray the following prayer with a clean conscience:

> Father in heaven, for the reasons I have listed, I will not leave the Masonic Lodge. I don't care that false gods are lifted up, or that it violates the holy scriptures. I don't care that it causes me to imitate pagan practices, or that it lowers the Lord Jesus Christ. And I don't care that it makes You equal to pagan gods, or the Holy Ghost to the Baphomet or the Devil. I think my reasons for staying are more important than Your reasons for me to leave. That is what I want, in Jesus' name, amen.

If you could really pray a prayer like that, let me ask you one more question. Could it be that you have never really trusted the Lord Jesus Christ as your Saviour—that you have never been born again?

I cannot imagine a Bible-believing Christian staying in such an ungodly organization, after understanding the facts clearly presented in this book. You would be doing what you know to be sin.

> Therefore to him that knoweth to do good,
> and doeth it not, to him it is sin. (James 4:17)

If you have not believed on Jesus Christ as your Saviour, now is the time to do it. "For all have sinned, and come short of the glory of God" (Romans 3:23). God's only begotten Son, the Lord Jesus Christ, shed His blood for you when He died on the cross. He paid for all your sins. You need to "call upon the name of the Lord" (Romans 10:13), admitting you are a sinner, and trust Him and His sacrifice alone to save you.

You may pray a prayer like this:

> Dear God, I am a sinner and need forgive-
> ness. I believe that Jesus Christ shed His pre-
> cious blood and died for my sin. I am willing
> to turn from sin. I now invite Christ to come
> into my heart and life as my personal Saviour.

You only have this life to put your trust in Christ.

> … it is appointed unto men once to die, but
> after this the judgment: (Hebrews 9:27)

There is no better time than now. Please do it today.

> … now is the accepted time; behold, now is
> the day of salvation   (2 Corinthians 6:2).